Is It
POWER
or
HATE

Is It
POWER
or
HATE

ESSAM ABOZID

ISBN: 1480195952

ISBN 13: 9781480195950

Library of Congress Control Number: 2012920508
CreateSpace Independent Publishing Platform
North Charleston, South Carolina

Printed in the USA.

TABLE OF CONTENTS

INTRODUCTION

Hate and war have existed throughout the history of humankind. Do Jews really hate Arabs or Arabs hate Christians or blacks hate whites or whites hate blacks? Does hate exist naturally between people and nations? How does hate originate? How and why is it being fed to people and by whom? We can answer these questions by examining what has occurred in our world and among the leaders and governments that have used hate in order to remain in power.

People and nations may hate one another due to personal experiences or due to other sources of information such as the media. When individuals and nations take in enough outside information, it can trigger the hate element in them, and they will discriminate against one another. They will go to war and kill one another for their own motivations and agendas, without regard for human rights or human value. It does not matter how old the victims are or whether they are children or adults. It does not matter whether they are men or women, black or white, Arabs or Jews. The warmongers do not see any difference; they only focus on achieving their goals.

Hate is not innate. It is formed from experience. Over time, external information in large doses can activate the "hate factor." Hatred and discrimination lead to war, death, and a disregard for human life. People will go to great lengths to protect their interests, regardless of the consequences to other people or groups. The common denominator is the underlying needs of a group or individual, not the means by which those needs are met.

What has been the true nature of hatred and exploitation over the course of history? Has it been true hatred, or has hatred been rooted in power and control? Has it been based on a need for certainty? Has it been based on a need to be considered significant? These are powerful and important questions, as many ancient civilizations and empires have had a profound effect on our society and have formed the foundation of our modern world.

Power and control come at different levels and in various forms in our daily lives in workplaces and in government. Many individuals and organizations seeking power are willing to achieve it at any cost and by any means, and they will hold on to it for as long as possible.

The political information and observations in this book are used to support the ideas within. To clarify the philosophical and psychological concept of the book.

Chapter One

THE RELIGIOUS PERSPECTIVE

The following is an example for the quest of power from the religious perspective. Many nations or conquering empires have persecuted others based on their beliefs in order to execute power and control over those they conquer.

Religion has existed for thousands of years. It is a system of values and beliefs organized around various leaders and certain practices. Events that took place thousands of years ago have much in common with present-day events; the commonality is that people want their needs met.

Let's begin by looking at the Jewish faith. The Jewish prophet Moses received his message of the Torah from God. Some of the people of the time accused Moses of being the author of the Torah and the messenger of the Jewish

11

faith. When he appeared with his message, the leaders and the pharaoh of that time rejected him because they feared the loss of power. Although his messages may have been valuable and empowering to the people, the leaders held on to their positions by controlling their citizens and their own wealth and resources. This power was more important to the leaders than whether Moses's message might benefit the people.

The same holds true like for Jesus in the Christian faith and Mohammed in the Islamic faith. When Jesus came with the Christian message and Mohammed came with the Islamic message, the leaders and kings of that time rejected these spiritual prophets and their teachings and created doubts as to their credibility by using hate as a tool to cause conflict among the people.

Jesus showed the people that he was a prophet and messenger of God. An example of his miracles is the healing of the sick and the blind. His birth—from the Virgin Mary by the spirit of God—was a miracle. The leaders in

Jesus's time, however, did not accept him as a prophet and messenger for the same reason they did not accept Moses. They feared that the people would revolt and seize control.

The Islamic prophet Mohammed also shared messages that were potentially life changing. His messages suggested a way of life that would help people treat one another with fairness, respect, and kindness. He taught that we are all accountable for our actions. His messages helped people open their eyes and understand right versus wrong and good versus evil. His teachings unsettled the rulers and kings, so they suppressed his messages, often with violence.

Political leaders have used hatred to their advantage when seeking new power or when trying to maintain existing power. The more hate that exists, the more divided people become, and the more those in power maintain control. The degree of control depends on how desperate or needy the people are or how rewarding the perceived outcome may be.

Achieving power sometimes requires war, manipulation, killing, or all of these in order to eliminate obstacles or perceived threats. Leaders have used hatred to gain more power or to stay in power, both domestically and internationally. Has this phenomenon changed over time, or has it remained the same?

To answer this question, the following chapter focuses on examples of various ancient empires. I chose some of them because I'm sure many people can relate to them. They will make my points easier to understand, since all of these nations and empires existed thousands or hundreds of years ago and successfully remained in power for hundreds of years. Did these empires exist and remain in power for so long because they were based on noble morals and on helping the people and communities? Or were these empires merely building dynasties and accumulating wealth that came from the power they possessed?

Chapter Two

THE GREAT EMPIRES

Let's take a look at the oldest and most powerful empires that have changed and shaped the world. An empire is a government or nation that extends itself into many different territories. The main reason empires were established and expanded was to become larger and stronger. The leaders of ancient empires wanted the resources of the people and other lands. Their motivation was not based on hate, discrimination, race, or religion; rather, it was based solely on a desire for power.

I

THE PERSIAN EMPIRE

The Persian Empire, also known as the Achaemenid Empire (approximately 550 BC– 330 BC), was forged by Cyrus the Great after he conquered the Median Kingdom in 550 BC. Cyrus was the reigning king from 559 to 530 BC. In 539 BC, Cyrus and his army captured the city of Babylon The Persians helped free the Jewish slaves from Babylonian captivity. In 538 BC, Cyrus the Great gave the Jews permission to return to Yehuda Province to rebuild their temple. Although many Jews chose to remain in Babylon, the reconstruction of the second temple in Jerusalem was considered a significant event in Jewish history.

In approximately 507 BC, the Persian Empire was one of the wealthiest, largest, and most powerful nations of the time. The Empire included the present day countries of Iran, Afghanistan, Pakistan, Bulgaria, Greece, Turkey, Iraq, Saudi Arabia, Jordan, Israel, and Egypt.

From 522 to 486 BC, the empire was under the rule of Darius I. By conquering other lands, the Persian Empire accumulated great riches. The religion of the Persians was Zoroastrianism. The Persians did not, however, interfere with the religions and customs of those whom they ruled over. Darius III was the ruler in 331 BC when Alexander the Great invaded the Persian territory.

II

THE GREEK EMPIRE

Prior to 336 BC, the Greek lands were comprised of a group of city-states that had no real political ties to one another. In 477 BC they formed the Dalian League under the leadership of Athens. The reason they came together was to join forces against the Persians. The league was disbanded in 404 BC after the war "the Greco-Persian war" ended.

Tensions arose between the Greek city-states and continued for many years. Sparta, Thebes, and Athens struggled for military and political power. The kingdom of Macedonia, under Philip II, however, rose to power, overcame the Greeks, and formed the League of Corinth. When Philip was assassinated in 336 BC, his son Alexander took over as king.

The Greek Empire lasted from 336 BC to 30 BC, beginning with the reign of Alexander. In 334 BC, Alexander took control over the Persian Empire. He then continued his campaign and went on to invade other territories. In 331 BC, he overthrew Darius III and conquered Babylon, which thrived as a center of commerce and learning. He died in Babylon in 323 BC. In just thirteen years, Alexander the Great had carved out an empire that extended from Greece to Egypt to Central Asia to India. After he died, the empire was divided among his four generals the empire lasted until 30 BC; the empire was then defeated by the Romans.

III

THE ROMAN EMPIRE

In 60 BC, Julius Caesar was elected as a roman general and became part of a triumvirate that included Pompey and Crassus. General Pompey seized Jerusalem in 63 BC and made it a client of Rome "was important to the Roman empire politically, economically" Caesar, who was extremely ambitious, went on a campaign to conquer the Gaul's. In 44 BC, he assumed leadership but was soon murdered. For the next thirteen years, Marc Antony and Octavian were consuls who contended for power. Antony sided with Cleopatra and the Egyptians, who were later defeated. Antony and Cleopatra both committed suicide. Marc Antony stabbed himself with a sword because he was ashamed of his military defeat. Cleopatra let herself be bitten by a poisonous snake because Egypt was going to be taken over by Rome, and she was going to be taken to Rome as a slave The Roman Empire lasted from 27 BC to AD 416, beginning with Augustus Caesar (Octavian) assuming the title of emperor. Augustus Caesar, was the first roman emperor, he ruled until his death in AD 14 Tiberius succeeded him. Over the course of its history, Rome experienced a succession of emperors.

In AD 6, Judea" now is Jordan, Palestine and Israel" became a Roman province after the death of King Herod. The Jews revolted against the Romans in AD 66 and then again in AD 115 and 132. Generals were appointed to crush the rebellions, and many Jews were killed or sold into slavery. With the final revolt, the Romans seized complete control of Jerusalem and expelled the Jewish people The emperor Constantine ruled from AD 306 until his death in 337.He founded Constantinople as a capital city in AD 330. In AD 312, he declared Christianity as the official religion of the Roman Empire. By AD 395, the Roman Empire had split into two parts, the Western and the Eastern or (Byzantine) Empires. By AD 410, the Roman Empire encompassed North Africa, the Middle East, parts of India, Russia, Central Asia, Western Europe, France, Belgium, and Germany.

After a series of attacks by northern and northeastern invaders, the Roman Empire fell to the conquerors by Gaul's army and the Barbarians army The Western Empire officially came to an end in AD 476, while the Byzantine Empire continued intact from the Western Roman Empire during late antiquity. The Byzantine Empire, also known as the Eastern Roman Empire, continued for more than a thousand years until 1453.

IV

THE ISLAMIC EMPIRE

The Islamic Empire expanded beyond the Arabian Peninsula after the death of the prophet Mohammed in AD 632. The Empire lasted until 1492. After it lost the war in Spain, the Islamic Empire was followed by the Turkish Empire, also known as the Ottoman Empire. Endured for centuries and only ended in 1924 when Ataturk founded the modern country of Turkey. The Islamic Empire stretched from the western border of China to southern France, Sicily, North Africa, and Central Asia.

After Mohammed's death, four of his closest followers, called caliphs, were elected to take charge. There was a dispute over the legitimacy of these leaders, however, which created religious and political unrest.as a result of this unrest. Islam was divided into two factions, the Sunnis and the Shia. The Sunnis became the major group of Islamic worshipers, and the city of Baghdad became the capital of the Muslim world.

From AD 632 to 642, Muslim armies seized control of parts of Egypt, Syria, Palestine, Mesopotamia, North Africa, Persia, and the Byzantine Empire. In the 600s, the ruling classes of East and West Africa converted to Islam. In 638 the Islamic Empire seized Palestine from the Byzantines. In 711, Arab armies invaded Spain, adding to the Islamic Empire's territorial expansion.

The Islamic Empire was not, however, solely expanded through war. On occasion, the Arabs were a welcome change for people who had been living under religious persecution and high taxes. Arab armies conquered most of these lands because people were attracted to Islam. The new religion did not force people to convert, and many people remained Jewish or Christian.

In 1453, the Ottomans overtook the city of Constantinople, which brought an end to the Byzantine Empire. The city was renamed Istanbul. The Ottoman Empire was tolerant of religions other than Islam. In 1922, Ataturk took over the mainland of Turkey and abolished the caliphate.

V

THE BRITISH EMPIRE

The growth of the British Empire reached its peak in 1920. The United Kingdom had acquired more than a quarter of the world's land, including highly populated territories in Asia, Africa, Canada, Australia, New Zealand, South Africa, and Hong Kong.

The British Empire began its growth in the late 1400s. In the early 1500s, it started to colonize the New World. By 1783, however, it had lost all thirteen colonies in North America after the War of Independence. Despite this setback, the British turned their attention toward Africa, Asia, and the Pacific.

In 1707 Scotland joined the parliamentary union to form the United Kingdom. In 1801 Ireland became part of the UK. The empire expanded further in 1851 as it acquired more territories and became a global industrial leader. With the growth of overreach and the war with Germany, however, the British economy had weakened.

By the end of the nineteenth century, there was military and economic tension between Germany and Britain, which contributed to the start of the First World War and placed an enormous financial strain on Britain. The Second World War further damaged and weakened the empire.

* * *

The empires described above had various backgrounds, regions, and religions. These empires invaded countries and nations, killing many civilians and soldiers in the process; they then gained power and maintained it they all did it for the same reasons. This is how these empires operated for thousands of years. Is this kind of power demand still happening in our society today?

We are living in a society with people who are presumably more educated and more civilized than ever. We expect to be ruled by leaders who advocate for democracy, justice, freedom, respect, fairness, and open dialogue, and we desire liberty and equality. Using military power to achieve world domination and show superiority is an undesirable action for those it affects. It simply creates more hate, generates more enemies, and produces further atrocities.

This is especially true with the technology that exists today. The entire world is more connected and more sophisticated than ever. This access to technology may put our enemies in even more powerful positions.

The underlying theme is power. The techniques used to gain power today may be more advanced and require more preparation, but the end result is the same. As always, the benefits and rewards from achieving this power only profit a small group of people.

How and why did empires in history form, and why were they in power for so long? If past events are any indication, these empires were not based on morals, nor were they formed to serve the greater good. The priorities were to build dynasties and acquire wealth that came from the power the empires possessed.

Chapter Three

CORPORATE POWER

A corporation is a body of combined and organized power. Corporations have the legal power to represent one person or a group of people, and they have power and authority of their own. Corporate power is one of the strongest and most effective kinds of power that exists today.

Corporations are owned and operated by the world's wealthiest people, those who are able to influence almost all major political decisions of most countries. They all have their own strategies and tactics they use to achieve what they want. The major players among corporations are those involved with the military, the oil industry, and the media.

I

MILITARY INDUSTRIAL POWER

Without conflict and war, there wouldn't be much need for the existence of the military because the military wouldn't be able to profit. Everyone would live in peace, and all regimes would feel safe and confident. If the regimes felt that ownership and power came from the rewards of freedom, democracy, and justice, our world might be quite different. A great superpower might achieve this by leading by example and transparency.

Many militaristic regimes exist in different parts of the world, including Asia, Africa, the Middle East, and South America. These areas are mostly dominated by a dictatorship that rules its people with an iron fist. These dictatorships buy weapons to fight and kill people, even their own people, just to stay in power. If these regimes believed they could rule the people by promoting a better way of life for every citizen, they would not have so many problems. In addition, if these countries respected the boundaries and sovereignty of other countries and treated one another with justice and respect, no matter how large or small each country is, peace would reign Some might argue that countries need weapons for self-defense from outside aggression. This is true but for only this reason: the sale of weapons is a moneymaking business; it protects the people on one side and kills people on the other. Two different needs are met. However, is killing people the main reason behind this kind of business? Are weapons sold because people hate people, or are they sold to make more money and allow governments to acquire more power, both domestically and internationally? Military manufacturers do not discriminate against one nation or another. Thus, weapons manufacturers continue to profit and maintain power through the vehicle of hate.

II

OIL COMPANIES

The oil business is extremely profitable. Oil is a natural resource that allows those who control it to lead the world's economy. Some countries have more access to oil than others. Oil also comes in different forms; while oil usually requires filtration, some countries have better-quality oil than others. In these instances, to extract oil from the ground, it need only be pumped. This requires much less work and expense, which makes its acquisition more rewarding Most large oil fields are located in the Middle East and North Africa, and they attract investors and oil companies. To secure their business, companies need to get control over the oil fields Achieving this often requires getting involved in the political arena because doing so helps elevate these companies into power. In turn, that power over the oil fields gives them a controlling factor in much of the world's economy, which helps nations generate even more power All countries depend on oil and oil products. The oil business can lead to war and aggression, with world leaders vying for control of the fields. Oil companies benefit from war because it generates money and power. During wartime, the average person does not obtain money and power; in fact, he or she experiences the opposite. We see this in our day-to-day lives with the rising prices of gasoline.

An example of how the oil business can be directly involved in war; was the situation with Iraq and Saddam Hussein. Oil companies, with help from the media, had to create enough reason for the US government to invade Iraq in the name of freedom for the Iraqi people. The goal was to replace Saddam Hussein with a new, more pro–United States government. In return US corporations would have more control over the oil fields.

All of this took place without consideration as to how many people from either side might die or suffer. The war did not stem from a natural hatred for humanity; rather, it was a way for corporations and leaders to achieve their goals at any price and by any means.

III

MEDIA POWER

The media play an important role in our lives, and many of our decisions depend upon the information provided by the media. The media can influence us to love or hate people or nations. Political and religious leaders as well as special-interest groups use mainstream media outlets to spread their messages.

This happens all the time, particularly during elections. Political candidates degrade and attack the credibility of their opponents with the hope of being elected. They use negative advertising against one another to achieve this.

The messages presented may be true or false. If they are false, people are being misled and will likely make uninformed decisions. Individuals only can make decisions based on the information provided. If the media feed society with distorted information, people will make decisions that do not serve the greater good. This presents a potential danger, both domestically and internationally.

The media are feeding tubes for love and hate, and they work in conjunction with other entities and individuals, especially political and religious leaders who use media "tubes" worldwide to mercilessly gain and maintain power. The race to obtain power always has existed and always will, from local political contests to the quest for world domination.

Control and wealth are the cornerstones of power. They speak to the basic human need that we have for certainty and significance in today's world. The media's power to deliver information is very strong. It is arguably more forceful than any other source of power because it sets the stage for all that can be accomplished by manipulating and misleading people's minds and opinions.

I mentioned the example of the war in Iraq above because the media played a major role in presenting the reason the US government went to war there, and it was later discovered that the information was false.

Other recent examples of the media presenting false information include:

- the lie about the Jessica Lynch story, discussed in chapter 4
- misinformation about the Benghazi attack in Libya on September 11, 2011, which killed US ambassador Christopher Stevens and three other Americans and about which congressman Dana Rohrabacher and Senator John McCain made some comments intended as

"proof" of deception or incompetence by the Obama administration in order to downplay the true nature of the Benghazi attack before election time For us as citizens, we rely on the information the media provides us. There is no other alternative. What this mean is if any media outlet have any special interest or any specific agenda they wanted to achieve if they presented to the public over and over again. The people after all will start to believe it as true. Because many people believe that the media should presented the true, honesty and reliable information and that's how it should be but unfortunately in many cases this won't happen

Chapter Four

CRISIS AND CONFLICT

A well-known crisis worthy of discussion is the Israeli-Palestinian conflict over the Israeli occupation of the Palestinian land. The Jewish people have existed for as long as any people of any other faith. They have contributed to society in many ways that have shaped the world we live in today. They have contributed to every civilization and community, including those in the Middle East, Africa, Asia, Europe, and North and South America. Despite all of their efforts and contributions, however, they never have been given due credit for their achievements as a Jewish nation or state. Instead they are credited as being an average people. Because they never have had an empire, I refer to the Jews as the Invisible Empire.

The Jews did not have their own land or a place to call home. For thousands of years How could a people or nation exist without a home or land Finally, after many centuries of living on different continents and helping other nations build their own civilizations, the Jews decided to build their own nation and own home.

In the late 1800s the Jewish people started a movement called Zionism to create a sense of unity. Between 1881 and 1914, thousands of Jews settled in Palestine. Most of them were from Eastern Europe. The Jewish people chose the land of Palestine not out of hatred for Palestinians but because the land was sacred to them. They sought a home of their own in 1948 the Jewish people established the state of Israel within the Palestinian land.

The question is why the Jewish people chose Palestine in particular. It is a very complicated matter, and the history of this part of the world has spiritual significance to Muslims, Christians, and Jews. All three of these major religions were born in this part of the world. This may be why this crisis is unique and complex. The Muslims' and Jews' claim to this territory inevitably leads to conflict in the name of religion.

The dispute over Palestine does not necessarily boil down to a question of who is good and who is evil. Every nation and religion has its own homeland except the Jewish people. They chose this land based on their special interests and heritage. From here the conflict started in the region and continues to this day.

Establishing the state of Israel or the Jewish state on this land should not be considered wrong or unjust if both sides are able to live in peace and harmony. Since this land is the mother of all three religions, and since Abraham is the father of all prophets, it would make sense that people should be able to share the land and live in peace and harmony.

The Jews did not choose to settle in this area out of hatred for Muslims or Palestinians. They simply wanted a home; they wanted a place for themselves. Building a home or country is not undertaken solely on the basis of hate, discrimination, or injustice but rather on the geographic and historical meaning of that nation. The Jewish leaders took all of these factors into consideration and used them to their advantage. Establishing their own home gave them a sense of security and more power to shape their own destiny. The same like any other nation, the more security they obtain the more power they have.

As for the Palestinians, are they victims of Israeli aggression and occupation? If the Palestinians and Jews were capable of living side by side, there might be less conflict. Since this is currently not the case, where would the Palestinian people go, and what might their future hold? Could they immigrate to another country? If so, what would become of their identity? Only time will tell what will happen.

I

THE COLD WAR

The point of my writing this book is to express that the underlying reason for all of these crises related to territorial disputes is not hatred, as it would appear to be, especially in the Middle East. The main reasons is a desire for power and control, as I illustrated earlier, using the British Empire as an example. The British Empire eventually weakened, and the United States and Soviet Union strengthened after the Second World War.

From then on, the world was divided. Into two superpowers, with each power racing to occupy and control more countries or offering them help in order to gain loyalty and power. The more countries these superpowers helped, the more support they received, and the more powerful they became. The two superpowers competed against each other using their military technology and economic power. Each one tried to get more allies from different parts of the world. The United States and the Soviet Union wanted these allies on their side in order to strengthen their own economy and make them stronger and more powerful These nations also accused each other of spying and stealing information. The Soviet Union was known as a communist country, and the United States viewed it as an evil nation. Indeed, during the Cold War when someone in the United States did something unpatriotic or unlawful, that person was sometimes referred to as a communist, which meant being disloyal or evil. The same phenomenon is occurring today with the word *terrorist,* which has become both significant and threatening, as the word *communist* During the Cold War, which lasted from 1945 to 1991, the United States and Soviet Union competed and combated against each other for world domination. Prior to this, they had one enemy in common: Nazi Germany. The United States and the Soviet Union were temporarily united and fought side by side to defeat the Germans during World War II. The war was divided into four zones among the United States, Russia, England, and France.

After the Germans and the other Axis powers were defeated in 1945, the mistrust between the United States and the Soviet Union intensified, sparking the beginning of the Cold War and contributing to the rise of the two superpowers.

The Soviet Union dominated and controlled China, Cuba, Romania, Albania, and Yugoslavia. The United States moved toward the Western countries of New Zealand, South

Africa, and Australia, as well as most countries in South America. Although political conflict, military tension, and economic competition existed between the two superpowers, their military forces never clashed directly. Instead they launched proxy wars, espionage, and nuclear arms races. The proxy wars they supported included the Korean War, the Berlin Crisis, the Vietnam War, the Cuban Missile Crisis, and the Soviet war in Afghanistan. All of these occurred to show the other what each was capable of.

The Korean War between North and South Korea lasted from June 1950 to July 1953. The Soviet Union supported the North, and the United States supported the South. This same scenario occurred during the Vietnam War; the United States supported the South, and the USSR supported the North.

During the Cuban Missile Crisis, the Soviet Union decided to build ballistic nuclear missiles in Cuba that had the ability to reach and strike the United States. This action was in response to the US missile bases in Italy and Turkey that had the capability to reach and strike the Soviet Union.

At the end of the 1970s, the Afghan War began, pitting the Soviets against the Mujahedin resistance. "Mujahedin are multi- national insurgent groups" The Soviet troops went in and seized control of a major government, military building and media building in order to take over Afghanistan.The Mujahedin, however, found help and support from various countries, including Egypt, Pakistan, Saudi Arabia, the United States, and the United Kingdom. Ultimately the Soviet Union lost the war in Afghanistan.

The initial Soviet deployment in Afghanistan began on December 2, 1979, and the final troop withdrawal started on May 15, 1998. The war lasted nearly nine years and ended on February 15, 1989. The Afghan War is an example of one of the proxy wars that took place in various parts of the world and that was supported by the two superpowers. As with other proxy wars, one power helped one country and the other power helped another country.

Under the Reagan administration, the United States increased diplomatic, military, and economic pressure on the Soviet Union. In order to end the cold war while that country was already suffering economic woes. Mikhail Gorbachev had a good relationship with Ronald Reagan and introduced liberalization, reforms, and reorganization of the government.

In 1991 the Cold War ended between the United States and the Soviet Union. The war had lasted almost forty-six years. Two years later, the Soviet Union dissolved into separate states and officially collapsed. This left the United States as the sole superpower and dominant military power in the world The Cold War has had a significant impact on the world today. During this time there was much suffering and death. Advancements in the media exacerbated the situation. Both the United States and the Soviet

Union used the media to demonize each other in order to get support from their own citizens. Both superpowers spent a great deal of money on their military forces and weapons. No citizens from either side benefited from this war.

During times of war and crisis, the cost of living rises, making it difficult for the average person to live a comfortable life. When a nation goes to war, a great deal of pressure is placed on the economy. The ones who make economic decisions are, of course, the political leaders from both sides. Again, the cause of war between the two countries was not hatred. Rather it was a race between two sides to become the world supreme power.

II

THE IRAQI-IRANIAN WAR

During the Afghan War, another war was underway in the Middle East, the Iraqi-Iranian War, which took place from 1980 to 1988. The war began when Iraq invaded Iran by air and land after a long history of border disputes.

In 1979, Iran had an Islamic revolution against Mohammed Reza Shah, the president of Iran. Later, the opposition was led by Ayatollah Khomeini. In February of 1979, the new leader,

Ayatollah, declared victory, and he made Iran into an Islamic republic instead of a monarchy Meanwhile, in the neighboring country of Iraq is Saddam Hussein. He and his government were afraid, that the Shia Muslims in Iraq would be influenced by the revolution in Iran, because the Shia, are the majority and they would have revolted against him. Unlike the majority of Iraqis, who were Shia Muslim, Hussein was a Sunni Muslim. However, Hussein had the Shia population under tight control.

Iraq wanted to gain control over the Gulf area by taking advantage of the chaos of the revolution occurring in Iran, so it attacked Iran without warning. Iran quickly regained all of its lost territory by June 1982. The war inflicted significant damage upon both Iran and Iraq in terms of deaths and each nation's economic stability. Almost a half-million Iraqi and Iranian soldiers and civilians are believed to have died in this war, with many more seriously injured.

The war in Afghanistan ended in 1989 and the war between Iraq and Iran ended in 1988. After many years of war, no changes were made in regard to the border rights of either region.

III

CONFLICT IN KUWAIT

By 1990 the Iraqi regime was involved in another war in Kuwait, and by 1991 the Soviet Union collapsed. Was this a coincidence? Or was it a well-planned strategy for Third World domination by the superpowers? This would result in control of the Middle East and remap the whole region by controlling the resources of the Middle East, by doing so they can control the global economy, and this is power.

In August 1990, during the first Gulf War (also known as Operation Desert Storm), the Iraqi regime invaded its neighbor Kuwait. Prior to this invasion, Saddam Hussein had had a decent relationship with the United States, which had supported him for eight years during his war with Iran. This was a war that left the Iraqi government economically shattered and in debt to Saudi Arabia.

Later, Saddam Hussein refused to pay his country's debt to the Saudis, claiming that he had gone to war with Iran to protect Saudi Arabia from the Iranian shah. He had to act in order to regain his power and recover from the devastation and defeat of the war with Iran. His chosen method of regaining power was to pick a fight with Kuwait. Prior to invading Kuwait Saddam Hussein had made his case against Kuwait publicly to the United States, Saudi Arabia, and other countries. He claimed that Kuwait was an Iraqi land that belonged to Iraq. He also warned that if the Kuwaiti government did not stop taking more than its fair share of oil, Iraqi troops would invade Kuwait and Kuwait City. Although he said this to April Glaspie, the US ambassador in Baghdad at the time, he was not taken seriously. He was told that this was an Arab-versus-Arab conflict that should be resolved between the two entities and that the United States would not take a position in the growing border dispute between Iraq and Kuwait. Saddam Hussein interpreted this as meaning that Glaspie was giving the green light for him to invade Kuwait, and less than a week later, he did.

Since the Iraqi regime had a fairly amicable relationship with the United States, the US government did not seem concerned about the conflict with the Kuwaiti government. Saddam Hussein operated as though it were acceptable to invade and take control of Kuwait City. Very quickly, however, the United States and Great Britain moved in to rescue the Kuwaiti people from the Iraqi regime by leading a coalition of thirty-four countries from around the world. By

March 1991, Kuwait once again had sovereignty and a government, this time under the protection of the United States.

As a result of Hussein's invasion of Kuwait, the United Nations passed a resolution to impose economic sanctions via a "no-fly zone" on Iraq. It also instituted the Oil-for-Food Program, under which the Iraqi government was allowed to sell just enough oil to buy food and medicine for the Iraqi people to survive. The United Nations passed another resolution called the UN Weapons Inspection Program, which allowed the United Nations to enter Iraq at any time to inspect for nuclear weapons. The purpose of this program was to make certain Iraq had no advanced nuclear weapons that would be a threat to the country's neighbors or to world security.

It was a mistake for the Iraqi regime to invade Kuwait City. It actually made Hussein weaker and put him and his people at greater risk. With the UN sanctions came economic setbacks and suffering for the Iraqi people. The sanctions lasted from 1991 to 2003, when the second Gulf War started.

Why did Saddam Hussein risk his position as the Iraqi president and cause mayhem and suffering for himself and the Iraqi people by going to war with Iran? Why did he take these steps if the neighbors he had conflicts with shared some of the same origins and the same religion as he? It's clear that his motivation was not driven by differences in color, race, or religion. He knew that if he succeeded in his mission of securing and controlling Kuwaiti and Saudi oil, Iraq would hold more power, not only in the Middle East but also in the global economy.

IV

PARALLELS BETWEEN EVENTS IN THE SOVIET UNION AND IRAQ

The main reason behind the Soviet Union's collapse was economic. These effects became apparent when the country went to war with Afghanistan, which put a great deal of economic pressure on the Soviet government. War kills people and drains governments and countries of their resources and wealth. By 1991, the Soviet Union had officially collapsed; soon after it was divided into smaller states and countries.

Was the collapse of the Soviet Union and the Iraqi regime predictable? It would appear so, as this can occur when a government gets involved in war and foreign affairs that do not serve its own people and economy. This is exactly what happened to the Soviet Union and Iraq, leaving the United States as the main superpower.

The United States saw a window of opportunity to step in and rescue the Kuwaiti government from Iraqi aggression and invasion; the US government knew that doing so would further enhance the relationship between the US and Kuwaiti governments.

What might have happened if Saddam Hussein and the Iraqi regime had chosen not to invade Kuwait? Would it have made any difference? The invasion gave the United States a reason to build a military base in the Middle East to maintain the peace in the area, which gave the United States more power.

V

THE TERRORIST ATTACK ON THE UNITED STATES

On September 11, 2001, the United States was attacked on its own soil. The attack took place on the World Trade Center (also known as the Twin Towers) when two hijacked jets were deliberately flown into the Twin Towers. This caused the towers and some of the surrounding buildings to collapse. As result almost 3000 people were killed, including the 227 civilians and 19 hijackers. The destruction of the Twin towers and the surrounding building caused serious damage to the American Economy, and also had significant effect on global markets. This was a result of closing Wall Street, the world financial district, until September, 17, 2001. The hijackers also intentionally crashed another plane into the Pentagon in Arlington, Virginia. The plane caused a partial collapse of the western side of the building. The fourth plane was targeted at Washington, DC. But crashed into a field near by Shanksville, Pennsylvania.After the passengers tried to overcome the hijackers. The attack resulted in terrible damage to the US economy, as well as to the country's relationship with Arab and Muslim nations.

According to the official investigation and eyewitness reports, those who launched this attack were members of al-Qaida, a Muslim group based in Afghanistan. The attack was not only devastating to the United States but also to the entire world, and many countries felt the pain and suffering of the American people. Nations around the world condemned the attack and supported the US government in its retaliation against those who were responsible for it.

The United States and other countries built a coalition to join forces against the attackers (al-Qaida). Although the attackers originated in Afghanistan, al-Qaida members exist in various countries all over the world. Accordingly, the United States declared war on al-Qaida so that it could locate them in any country.

The United States declared that if any countries supported terrorists by supplying them with funds or shelter, they too would be on the terrorist list and considered enemies of the United States. President George W. Bush famously said, "You are either with us or against us." The result was the creation of the New World Order. In effect, all countries were now under the supervision of the United States; the option was to comply with the United States as an ally or fight it as an enemy.

The United States went to war in Afghanistan in retaliation for 9/11 and to defeat al-Qaida. The United States aimed to eliminate al-Qaida by disabling its ability to attack again. As of this writing, the war in Afghanistan is still continuing. It has been under way for more than ten years, and it seems as though there is no end in sight. The war has cost the United States many more lives and much more money than military experts predicted. As a result, the war has placed a tremendous strain on the US economy.

One of the most important reasons the United States went to war in Iraq was to replace the Iraqi regime and to complete the job of the first Gulf War. To proceed with the invasion of Iraq, the United States needed a compelling reason to remove the Iraqi president from power and replace him with a more democratic, more pro–United States regime.

The Bush administration used the power of the media to demonize the Iraqi regime. In so doing, they fostered hate not just in the hearts of Americans but also in the hearts of every person who saw and heard the news worldwide. By using hatred as a tool, the Bush administration gained the approval of the American people and people around the world to launch a war in Iraq, even though the war in Afghanistan was still taking place.

A prime example of media manipulation that occurred during the Iraqi war is the story of Jessica Lynch, a supply clerk in the US Army who was stationed in Iraq. On March 23, 2003, her convoy made a wrong turn in the city of Nasiriya, and Iraqi troops ambushed her and captured her. The Humvee that Lynch was driving was struck by a grenade, which caused the vehicle to crash, and she suffered severe injuries. She was taken to a hospital, in Iraq where she recovered, and was then rescued by US commandos. Lynch's story was then embellished by her and the media to make it appear that she had been terribly mistreated by the Iraqi troops, and the media turned her into a war hero. This allowed the American people to focus on Iraq as an enemy.

The war on Iraq was launched in part because the United States believed the Iraqi regime might be using chemical weapons on its own people. The United States also thought that Iraq had the capability to possess and use nuclear weapons. Furthermore, there was an association between the Iraqi regime and al-Qaida. The Iraqi regime was thought to be dangerous and might threaten the stability of the entire region, as well as the safety of the world. The world had to eradicate the Iraqi regime and Saddam Hussein immediately, according to the Bush administration and its allies.

In 2003 the United States and Great Britain declared war on Iraq to free the Iraqi people from the dictatorship of Saddam Hussein. The goal was to install a new democratic government and place the Iraqi nuclear weapons program under UN team inspection. Ultimately the United States seized control of Iraqi landand captured Saddam Hussein. He subsequently was removed from power, turned over to the courts, and accused of war crimes.

Hussein was found guilty and sentenced to death by public hanging on a Muslim holiday (Eid al-Adha). Also known as the Feast of the Sacrifice, this is a very important religious holiday for Muslims. The United States wanted to send a message to the entire world, not just to the Iraqi government and Hussein's regime. The message was that the United States has the power and ability to challenge and remove any regime that threatens its interest in any place in the world. This message aligns with President George W. Bush's famous phrase, "You are either with us or against us." It also confirms the New World Order and the fact that the United States is the sole superpower.

The US government stated that it invaded Iraq and removed Saddam Hussein due to concern that the country possessed weapons of mass destruction. Soon after the invasion of

Iraq, however, no evidence of chemical weapons or an advanced chemical program was found. In addition, there was no evidence of an association between Hussein and al-Qaida. Even so, thousands of people were killed and millions of dollars spent, which caused devastation, suffering, and a drain on the US economy.

Did the US government mislead its own people? Or did it make an honest mistake in accusing Iraq of having weapons of mass destruction? US military forces invaded Iraq while the United States was at war with Afghanistan. The war with Afghanistan should have taken priority as this is where al-Qaida originated. It should also be noted that while the 9/11 hijackers were affiliated with al-Qaida, most of them were Saudi Nationals. They were not from Afghanistan nor were they Iraqi, since the Saudi government one of the most important ally and player in the Middle East to the United States. It should help the United States to investigate this case to clarifier this atrocity. For the world history and for it's won future generation.

Did the Bush administration demonize the Iraqi regime to win the support of the American people? Did Bush expect the entire world to follow and support him in going to Iraq to finish the war that had been on hold since 1991 (Operation Desert Storm) or the liberation of Kuwait City?

The Bush administration went back to Iraq in 2003 to complete the mission and to secure US power in the Middle East. Keep in mind that after the United States helped free the Kuwaiti people from the Iraqi regime, it won the trust of the Kuwaiti government and people. It also won Kuwaiti oil for US oil corporations.

Since the United States had an amicable relationship with the Saudi government, it did not want to jeopardize this relationship, even though the 9/11 hijackers had been identified as Saudi citizens. In the future; however, if the relationship changes the United States might confront the Saudi government.

Another reason the United States confronted Iraq rather than Saudi Arabia is that the US oil companies wanted to keep the Iraqi oil fields under control, and that could only happen through invasion and removal of the Iraqi regime from power. Doing so gave US commanders control and power in the Middle East as well as the entire world. For oil companies and lobbyists, that is true power.

Gaining that kind of power was Hussein's idea from the very beginning, but the United States prevented him from doing so. The US government adopted this strategy itself and executed it to achieve what every leader or empire wants—more power. The United States did not specifically hate the Iraqi people or Saddam Hussein. At one time Hussein had a good relationship with the United States. Circumstances, however, changed, and when the time came for gaining more power, an enemy was created. It just happened to be the Iraqi regime at the time.

The Bush administration used the power of the media to demonize the Iraqi regime in order to create fear, which generates hate. The administration used hate as a vehicle for power, and fear was the fuel that kept the vehicle going. Fear and hate are emotions, and emotions drive our decisions. It's easy to control people's emotions and decisions if the media is on your side. Leaders and nations that seek more power do not discriminate against any group in particular. Everyone is equal. The power seekers will destroy anyone who gets in their way or opposes or threatens them or their interests.

Chapter Five

ACTION AND POLICY

During times of war and crisis, political leaders sometimes use phrases and words that come from a religious perspective. For example they might declare, "This is a holy war," or, "This is a crusade" to convince people that they will fight on their behalf. They hope to gain power. Average citizens, however, pay the price of war and crisis, while political leaders gain more power and wealth. They tell their citizens they are going to war because their religion is under attack or they are seeking more justice and freedom. Political leaders need support and approval to go to war or to launch an attack. In the end, the leaders are the only beneficiaries, not the public.

I

AMERICAN POLICY

Since the World Trade Center attackers happened to be Arab-Muslim, the US government decided to take measures against the Muslim people, especially those from the Middle East. American policy changed toward the Muslim people after 9/11. This can be seen by increased scrutiny and security measures of flights originating in the Middle East or other Muslim nations. Another example is surveillance of civilian telecommunications. The goal of these changes is to prevent any future attacks. In addition, not only the United States but also the entire non-Muslim world seems to be at war with Muslims. Much of the world felt that the attack on the World Trade Center was unjustified, and they stood behind the United States and supported it as a world leader and supreme power. It is important to realize, however, that al-Qaida is just one sect and does not represent the entire Islamic nation.

With all of the actions and policy changes toward Muslims and Arabs, can one infer that the United States hates Muslims and Arabs? Of course is not. This policy change happened in retaliation for 9/11 to show the world that United States is still the only superpower.

The events that unfolded after 9/11 are similar to the events that occurred during the Cold War. The Soviets were the primary enemy of the United States because both countries were racing to power. After the fall of the Soviet Union, the relationship between the United States and Soviets now is better than before. But keep in mind that the cold war it could be resurrected again at any time. Because of this the United States won the competition and became the sole superpower. The focus now is on the Middle East, and the US government considers some of Middle Eastern countries to be its enemies, or not pro-American. Much as Russia, Cuba, and Vietnam once were. So again, conflicts between nations are not about hate or religious beliefs, but about power.

In the past, the United States has had conflicts with Christian nations, including Germany, Vietnam, North Korea, Cuba, and Nicaragua. Today, however, the focus has shifted to the Middle East and to extending power and control to a region that is rich with many resources. Whoever controls the area's resources controls the world economy, which means gaining and maintaining power.

Once the war on Islam ends and the United States has full control, the relationship may change. The United States may become friendly with the Arabs, just as it did with Russia, and the United States and the Islamic nations may reconcile one day with each other as two candidates do after an election. They are currently demonizing each other, but once a winner is declared, they will unite.

II

ISRAELI-PALESTINIAN POLICY

As for the Israeli-Palestinian conflict, who will vanish and who will prevail? The more powerful country is most likely to survive, and that will likely be the state of Israel. The scenario of two separate states for Palestine and Israel, in my opinion, will never happen—not now, not ever. This is because the dire conditions under which the Palestinians live may decrease the Palestinian population. Some people will die, while others may relocate to escape occupational attacks.

89

Whoever chooses to remain in Palestine will have to accept the fact that they are just a people who live within the state of Israel. This will give the Israeli government the right to own and control the entire land. The Israeli people will then be able to say that they have their own state. This will give them more of a feeling of power and security, which is what they want.

How or when will this happen? It does not matter. There is no time limit, as long as the goal and persistence are there. This is what is important. When the time is right, it will happen no matter how long will takes.

But there is another option. From what I have noticed, the most troubled area of Palestine for the Israeli is the Gaza Strip, especially now.

As I write this book, it has been little more than a year since Israel attacked the Gaza Strip on November 3, 2012. The attack was accelerated after both the Israeli and the Hamas governments accused each other of starting violent attacks. Hamas is a Sunni Islamic organization that controls and governs the Gaza Strip. This is not the only violence or attack. There has been ongoing atrocity on both sides, and it seems to have no end, in regard to the Gaza Strip in particular.

Therefore I would like to propose an idea or solution to this problem that would be fair, just, and agreeable for all parties involved in this situation.

I believe that with this solution, the Israeli people and their territory will be more safe and secure. The people of the Gaza Strip will also be more safe and secure. Plus, they will have the benefit of living freely with dignity and without fear of any future attacks from the Israeli army. Again, the solution has to be agreeable to all parties are involved: Egypt, Israel, and Gaza.

First let us look at the history of the Gaza Strip. The Gaza Strip acquired its current northern and eastern boundaries as a result of the 1948 Arab-Israeli war. These boundaries were confirmed by the Israeli-Egyptian armistice agreement on February 24, 1949, which stated that the Gaza Strip and the Palestinian government were to be governed and protected by the Egyptian government. Then in 1967, the Israelis seized the Gaza Strip from Egypt and occupied it in a six-day war. Until 2005 the Israeli army withdrew from the Gaza Strip. However, in 1993, the Oslo Accords were signed, and the Palestinian authority became the governor of the Palestinian population. As of July 2007, following the 2006, Palestinian elections, Hamas has taken over control of the Gaza Strip and split with Palestinian authority.

III

HERE IS MY IDEA:

The Israeli government should agree to modify the peace agreement with Egypt in a way that makes the Egyptian people happy, because Egypt could play a very important role in this conflict. That role is governing the Gaza Strip, just as Egypt did in the past.

This means that the Gaza Strip would be another state of the Egyptian territory. Therefore, there would be no more underground tunnels and no more weapons smuggling from outside of Gaza that puts the Israeli at risk of violence and rocket attacks. The Gazan people would have no need for smuggling anything because they would be living with Egyptian brothers. On the other hand, Egypt would have to move its security forces to the border between the Gaza Strip and Israel to monitor the border and keep it free from violence and terrorists.

I think this solution is agreeable and doable if all parties act in good faith and are serious about doing the right thing for their own citizens and humanity to stop this crisis once and for all.

IV

THE ARAB AUTUMN

As we observe events unfold in the Middle East, we see revolutions and regime changes taking place in areas such as Tunisia, Egypt, and Libya. The various regimes have suppressed their own people and misused their power and their own wealth. They have created poverty, desperation, and hopelessness among the people. To remain in control, they've had to keep people divided by creating problems and fostering hate. They have kept the people busy fighting so that the people will not see the corruption taking place.

The Egyptian revolution began on January 25, 2011, when President Hosni Mubarak was asked to resign by the majority of the Egyptians. The Egyptians also demanded that the constitution be revised. They asked for more freedom and democracy, and a time limit on the presidency. The revolution ended on February 11, 2011, when President Mubarak stepped down after almost thirty years in office. The Egyptian people had won the fight and removed Mubarak from power. However, up to now the future of Egypt is still in jeopardy. This is true for the entire Arab region, not just in Egypt. I personally do not see a light at the end of the tunnel in the near future, the road to stability in the region will be long and winding. I hope that I am wrong.

Some people call what is occurring in the Middle East the "Arab Revolution", and some call it the "Arab Spring". I do not believe there is an Arab Spring for the Arab people. The term *spring* applies more in the West. The revolution started because the people were suppressed for so long. They wanted to be free and respected.

The Arab people desire social justice and a decent life for all. Some Western countries, however, benefit from this revolution more than the Arabs themselves, because in the midst of all the crises and chaos, some countries are seizing the opportunity to make money by selling weapons and financing the revolution on both sides. The longer the conflict lasts, the more money there is to be made. There is no motivation for those countries outside of the Middle East to end the conflict, as long as this is the case. Oil corporations are also taking advantage of the chaos, thinking they have a chance to seize oil fields under new regimes.

I refer to the situation in the Middle East as the "Arab Autumn." The uprising of the Arab nations, including Tunisia, Egypt, Libya, Syria, Yemen and Algeria against their own governments, may bring more chaos and destruction to the entire region. The various actors are fighting each other because they each, with their own interests, want to be in power, which could lead to civil wars.

V

THE AMERICAN DREAM

The United States is the only superpower in the world today. It is involved in multiple wars, which is stretching the American economy even thinner and making life more complex. The tax money that is being used to finance these wars would be much better spent on the people of the United States and on strengthening the economy rather than on weapons. This type of spending only benefits large corporations that "cash in" on the human tragedy, which could be considered, "Corporate greed."

The United States is still considered the greatest country in the world and the land of opportunity. People from around the world still dream about immigrating to the United States. These people often risk their lives to make it in to the United States so, that their families can have a chance at the *dream* and to secure a successful future.

The United States is blessed with resources and opportunities for anyone who wants to pursue them. In the United States, it does not matter, who you are or where you come from. Your level of success is limitless; this is not always the cases in other parts of the world. If you are hardworking, ambitious, persistent, and yearn for success, the opportunity is there for you to make it.

Unlike in most third world countries, a person living in the United States does not need to be concerned with their government intimidating and suppressing them, because of the laws which protect them from such actions.

The laws in United States strive to protect everyone equally and no one is above the law. This is another example of what makes this country so great.

The United States is truly the "land of the free," because so many people have the opportunity to transform their dreams in to reality. It is the responsibility of every person who lives in the United States, to do whatever it takes, to keep the dream alive for everyone. This includes protecting our nation from any harm. It is our responsibility as good Americans, to ensure the same opportunity exists for future generations.

As Americans, we are fortunate enough to have the opportunity to enjoy our freedoms and the ability to pursue and archive our personal goals, every day. We should not take this for granted, because there are still people around the world who are suffering and dying to gain the freedoms we have in their own homelands.

It is important to keep in mind and understand the perspective of immigrants, who choose to come to the United States, by their own free will. Immigrants make the choice to come to the United States, because they love and believe in the freedoms and rights afforded to people living in the US. What this conscience decision demonstrates, is their commitment to be patriotic to the US.

Just because a person is not born in the United States, it is important that we, as a society, do not pass judgment on or doubt the person's love or patriotism to the United States. Their love and belief in this country is just as real as someone who was born in the US. And while some people may eventually decide to return to their country of origin, they still value the freedoms and experience. These visitors often positively contribute to our society and culture during the time they were here.

VI

PRESERVING THE AMERICAN DREAM

Because of our position in the world, it is our responsibility to be aware of corrupt and careless politicians, in our government. We should be mindful of who is influencing our politicians – in particular when the influencers have a stake in or benefit from engaging in wars or conflicts. In these cases, politicians may be inclined to engaging in wars- with the intention of benefiting lobbyists and their agendas. It is our civic duty to stop these types of corrupt politicians by challenging them and using the power of our vote to get them out of office. I say this, because no good has come out any war. This is true not just for the United States, but around the world.

Careless politicians have dragged the US military from one war to another over the past decade – and it is important that this cycle ends as it is not sustainable. Engaging in long term wars has had a negative impact on the US which will likely be felt for generations to come.

The most devastating impact of long term wars is that they drain the economy and decrease job. Given this, I believe that if any nation chooses to engage in a long term war again in the near future, that this would be a recipe for economic disaster and collapse for the nation.

History tells us this is the case, because this approach was the main reason many of the ancient empires collapsed. We have to learn from those lessons in order to protect this nation from collapsing, before it is too late. We must do so by challenging corrupt politicians – it is the only we can keep this nation safe and strong.

Rather than engaging and spending money on wars, we should be investing that money in our economy here at home. This could be achieved by increasing investment in our natural resources and revitalizing the manufacturing industry. Pursuing the growth of "Made in America," will strengthen the economy and put millions of people to work.

Wars do not make money; they take money. Wars do not help achieve peace and security; they create enemies and inspire terrorism. Wars do not create jobs; they create unemployment and inflation.

I want to share the story of a recent conversation that I had with some colleagues that illustrates a common misconception that many people have about the "benefits of war." What began as casual conversation soon became a passionate debate about the pros and cons of engaging in war.

The argument that I made was that wars have a negative impact on the economy and causes negative "psychological" trauma to society. As a counter to my position, someone from the group suggested that wars are "actually good for the economy." This person supported their argument by saying that the world economy was stronger than ever during World War II.

I disagreed with him. Why did I disagree with him? Because the reality is that the economy improved only after the war ended. The post-World War II economic expansion, which was also known as the "post-war economic boom" or the "Golden Age of Capitalism," occurred *following* the end of World War II in 1945. This period of economic prosperity lasted until the early 1970's, but was then followed by numerous setbacks. These setbacks included the collapse of the Bretton Woods System in 1971, the oil crisis in 1973, and the stock market crash from 1973-1974; which led to the 1970's recession.

During the economic boom, there was high worldwide economic growth particularly, in the United States, Greece, West Germany, France, Japan, China, and Italy. These countries were able to recover quickly from the economic downturn by investing in their own infrastructure. I believe this is still the best solution for rebuilding the economy, today. This approach would improve the US economy and strengthen the value of the Dollar. This would then have a positive impact on the global economy given the role the United States' financial systems play in a time of increased globalization.

Regardless of who is in power today or tomorrow, what is most important is that the country that is considered to be the ultimate superpower, should lead by positive examples. The most powerful countries in the world should model justice, respect, honesty, and fair trade for the rest of the world. An example of this would be when, you work for someone, it doesn't matter who your boss is; you only care if that person respects you, treats you fairly, and pays you well.

CONCLUSION

All of the conflicts and revolutions in the Middle East provide proof enough of the significance of gaining power and control. Being in or maintaining power is the goal of, any nation; even if this comes at the cost of the lives of innocent people whom may even share the same religion and background as the aggressor. Each group believes it is right and that the other group is wrong. Both sides demonize each other in order to gain the advantage. They do this to manipulate the common people. It is not a matter of hate or discrimination; it is the need for power.

How can we change this pattern of behavior and make the world a better place and an open and free society for everyone? Dear readers, whether you are Arab or non-Arab, Jewish or Muslim, Christian or any other faith, you may be affected by the negative media or by any war. You may have been disenfranchised, victimized, or even labeled as a terrorist because of your background, ethnicity, religious beliefs, or ideological beliefs. However, those are your basic human rights, the right to freely pursue your beliefs without being victimized and they should be protected and promoted by our society and government. This is how it should be all over the civilized world.

Prejudice can cause you suffering, humiliation, and loss of your job, home, or family. You may sometimes feel that you have to hide your real identity or your ethnicity to conceal your beliefs in order to avoid discrimination or confrontation.

I would like to tell you that most wars, crises, and conflicts, if not all, are launched and occur for political reasons and political ambitions.

So you are very much a victim of political ambitions. It is nothing personal; it is not about hate. So what I believe you can do is to stand up tall and be proud of yourself and your heritage. Stand behind your beliefs and ideas. Do the best you can to serve society and your community. Be honest with the people you interact with, and be the best at what you do. Treat people with respect.

Most people are fair and understanding. If they notice all these positive characteristics in you, they will acknowledge you and may change their opinions of you. If they have negative opinions because of negative coverage, stories in the media. That are occurring, it is up to you to help them change their opinions.

As much as you believe the sun will come out tomorrow the troubles of today will work themselves out.

Now imagine everyone living freely and in peace. Imagine everyone coexisting in harmony

and decency. Imagine that the only way to iden-
tify a person is by name, not by religion, color,
or background.

What would it take to make this happen? It
would require people reaching out to help one
another while practicing peace, justice, and love.
Practicing these tenets could change a great
deal in the world. There is strength in unity and
cooperation. We could change the war zone to a
life zone, fear to security, deceit to honesty, and
domination to an open and free society. Is this
possible? Perhaps, but in the end, it all comes
down to power and control.

AUTHOR BIOGRAPHY

Essam Abozid is an entrepreneur and a businessman who has traveled extensively around the world. Through his various business endeavors, he has had the opportunity to meet and talk with many people.

As an American Muslim of Arab descent, Essam noticed a major change in the United States in the aftermath of the tragedy of September 11, 2001. This change was specifically among the American people and US policies toward Arabs and Muslims. He realizes these changes occurred even though only small groups of people were responsible for the attacks.

The attacks devastated the American population and its psyche as a whole. As a result of this tragedy, the entire Muslim population also is suffering, and many American Muslims feel they are being treated as second-class citizens. Some people believe they can prejudge Muslims as terrorists and point their fingers at Muslims for any terrorist act that occurs. This is what opened the door for Abozid to do some research and write this book.

Abozid wanted to learn why this tragedy occurred and why wars have occurred in general in modern times and throughout history. He also wanted to find out who the real beneficiaries of wars and crises are and to remind people not to prejudge a community or nation based on an atrocity that was committed by a small group of people. Abozid believes that we must judge people one person at a time and that this approach will allow us to fairly assess people's character. This comes from the acknowledgment of individuality and from personal experiences with people that we already know like our neighbors, co-workers, or even members of our own family.

www.ingramcontent.com/pod-product-compliance
Lightning Source LLC
Chambersburg PA
CBHW072324290526
45794CB00002B/737